Rubin,Susan Goldman   940.53
The Anne Frank Case   RUB

6/26/22	713	DATE DUE	

The Anne Frank CASE

Simon Wiesenthal's Search for the Truth

by SUSAN GOLDMAN RUBIN

illustrated by
BILL FARNSWORTH

Holiday House / New York

ONE NIGHT IN October 1958 at nine thirty, the phone rang in Simon Wiesenthal's apartment in Linz, Austria.

"Can you come at once to the Landes Theater?" asked a friend, who sounded upset.

Simon's friend told him that he was attending a performance of *The Diary of Anne Frank.* But it had been disrupted.

"Traitors! Swindlers!" a group of teenagers had shouted at the actors, booing and hissing. The show had stopped as demonstrators dropped leaflets from the balcony that read:

This play is a fraud. Anne Frank never existed. The Jews have invented the whole story because they want to extort more *restitution money*. Don't believe a word of it! It's a fake!

3

The situation demanded Simon's attention. Since the end of World War II in 1945, he had devoted his life to exposing the crimes of Nazis, the followers of Adolf Hitler. Simon's self-appointed mission was to educate the public, especially young people, about the Holocaust. The Holocaust was a campaign launched by Hitler, who had ruled Germany from 1933 to 1945, aimed at wiping out entire groups of people he considered inferior, such as Gypsies, or Roma; homosexuals; and most of all Jews, such as the teenaged Anne Frank.

Anne Frank wrote her diary in Amsterdam from June 1942 to August 1944 while hiding from Hitler's secret police, the *Gestapo*, in an annex along with family and friends. On August 4, 1944, the group of eight Jews were arrested when a Dutch informer tipped off the German police. Anne and the others were sent to *concentration camps*. Only Anne's father, Otto, survived the Holocaust. He had Anne's diary published. It was translated into many languages, becoming an international best seller, a stage play, and a movie. The diary touched readers and audiences everywhere. But in Linz, where Hitler had grown up and gone to school, many people refused to believe the Holocaust had happened.

By the time Simon arrived at the theater, the performance had resumed. The police were already there, taking down the names of several demonstrators from a local high school.

"When I arrived at the Landes Theater," recalled Simon, "the play had just ended, but groups of young people still stood around discussing the incident. I listened to them."

Many of the teenagers agreed with the *neo-Nazi* protesters that the Anne Frank story was a lie.

The next morning Simon visited the police station. The parents of the teenagers who had been arrested wanted to brush aside the whole matter. "It was just a few young people . . . having fun," they said.

Although Simon heard that the students would be disciplined at school, not one was punished. Simon realized the guilty ones were not only the kids "but their parents and teachers." After the war ex-Nazis had returned to their teaching jobs in Austria and Germany. Some remained silent about their past. Others boasted. Many ex-Nazis and Nazi sympathizers taught that the Holocaust had either never happened or that it had been greatly exaggerated. The adults were passing along a heritage of bigotry and ignorance to their children.

Two days after the neo-Nazi demonstration at the theater, everybody was still talking about the protest. At a coffeehouse with a friend, Simon spoke with a high-school boy his friend knew and had called over to them.

"Fritz," Simon's friend asked, "were you at the theater during the demonstration?"

"Yes, of course," said Fritz.

"Did you read those pamphlets?" he asked.

"They're true," said Fritz.

Simon's friend gestured toward him and asked, "Do you know who this is?"

"Yes. Wiesenthal the Nazi hunter." Word of Simon's work had spread throughout Linz and beyond. Sometimes mail came to him simply addressed "Wiesenthal, Austria."

Simon spoke to Fritz in a friendly voice. "What about Anne Frank's diary?" he asked.

Fritz shrugged. "The diary may be a clever *forgery*. Certainly it doesn't prove that Anne Frank ever lived," he said. "Anyone could get hold of an old exercise book and write something or other in it; anyone could 'find' that exercise book in an attic. There is no proof."

"Young man," Simon said to Fritz, "if we could prove to you that Anne Frank existed, would you accept the diary as genuine?"

Fritz said, "How can you prove it?"

"Suppose the Gestapo officer who actually arrested Anne Frank were found. Would *that* be accepted as proof?"

Fritz grinned. "Okay. *If* the man himself admitted to it. We'll accept it from him, but not from you."

At that very moment Simon took on a new case. "I had to find the man who had arrested Anne Frank fourteen years before."

Simon became a Nazi hunter because he himself was a Holocaust survivor. But before Hitler came to power, Simon had published political cartoons in magazines and newspapers. In 1932, after studying architectural engineering in Prague, Czechoslovakia, he designed houses in L'vov, which was then part of Poland. A few years later he married his high-school sweetheart, Cyla Muller.

But that happy period of his life came to an end when on September 1, 1939, the Nazis invaded Poland. Two weeks later the Soviet army also invaded, and World War II began.

First under the Soviet Union, then under Germany, Polish Jews lived with increasingly harsh rules. Simon could no longer work as an architect and became a mechanic in a bedsprings factory. Simon's widowed mother came to stay with him and Cyla.

In June 1941 the German army defeated the Soviets in L'vov. In the bloody victory celebration that followed, *Ukrainian* troops who had fled the Soviets and sided with the Germans arrested as many educated Jewish men as they could find. For three days they killed doctors, lawyers, teachers, and architects. Simon hid in a cellar but was captured. "We stood in a courtyard with our hands behind our heads," he recalled. "A man took a pistol and shot the people one after another." Just as it was Simon's turn, church bells rang out. It was six o'clock. "That's enough for today," said the soldier. And the soldiers stopped the executions to attend services.

The twenty Jews who were left were imprisoned. That night a policeman working for the Nazis recognized Simon. The man, a former assistant bricklayer who had worked for Simon, helped him escape.

A few days later Simon, his wife, and his mother were ordered to move to a sealed-off part of the city just for Jews, the *ghetto*. In October they were sent to the Janowska Concentration Camp, then transferred to a *forced-labor camp*, where they worked on the Eastern Railroad. Because of Simon's artistic skills, he was given a job creating posters and signs and painting *swastikas* and German eagles on captured locomotives.

His boss, Heinrich Guenthert, gave him special assignments in the railway repair shop. Here Simon met members of the Polish underground, who were secretly fighting the Nazis. He persuaded them to smuggle his wife out of the labor camp. With her blond hair, her greenish blue eyes, and a false passport, Cyla could pass for an *Aryan* and make it to Warsaw. Simon's supervisor, Nazi Chief Inspector Adolf Kohlrautz, signed the fake identification card for Cyla. But Simon could not help his mother. She was transported by freight car with hundreds of other old Jewish women to the Belzec Death Camp. He never saw her again.

Simon remained at the labor camp. On Hitler's birthday, April 20, 1943, it looked as though Simon would not survive, either. The *SS* (Hitler's protection squad that became a private army) took Simon and two other Jews back to Janowska. They lined them up with thirty-eight Jewish men and women, forced their prisoners to undress, and began to shoot them.

Just as it was Simon's turn, a whistle blew and someone called his name. "We need Wiesenthal," someone shouted. Simon couldn't believe he had been saved. Twice he had escaped death. They told him to get dressed and took him back to the railway works, where Kohlrautz was waiting for him. "We need him to finish the posters for the Hitler birthday celebrations," Kohlrautz told the SS officer. "For a long time," Simon said, "I was the only person I knew in the camps who still believed in miracles."

By September Kohlrautz not only let Simon know that Jews would soon be sent back to Janowska and shot, but he gave him a chance to escape. Sent by Kohlrautz to buy painting materials with a feeble-minded policeman as his escort, Simon ran out the back door of the store and was hidden by a member of the underground from the repair shop. After four days Simon escaped to the woods near L'vov.

Simon met up with *partisans* fighting the Nazis, who hid him under the floorboards of a house. Simon had paper and pencils. All during this time while he was hiding, he kept a diary and lists of SS guards and their crimes as well as lists of Nazis, such as Guenthert and Kohlrautz, who had behaved decently. "I wrote down everything I knew," said Simon. Simon had a phenomenal memory. He also made secret maps and drawings of the ghetto and concentration camps. All of these materials were seized on June 13, 1944, when the Gestapo found Simon under the floorboards of the house and arrested him.

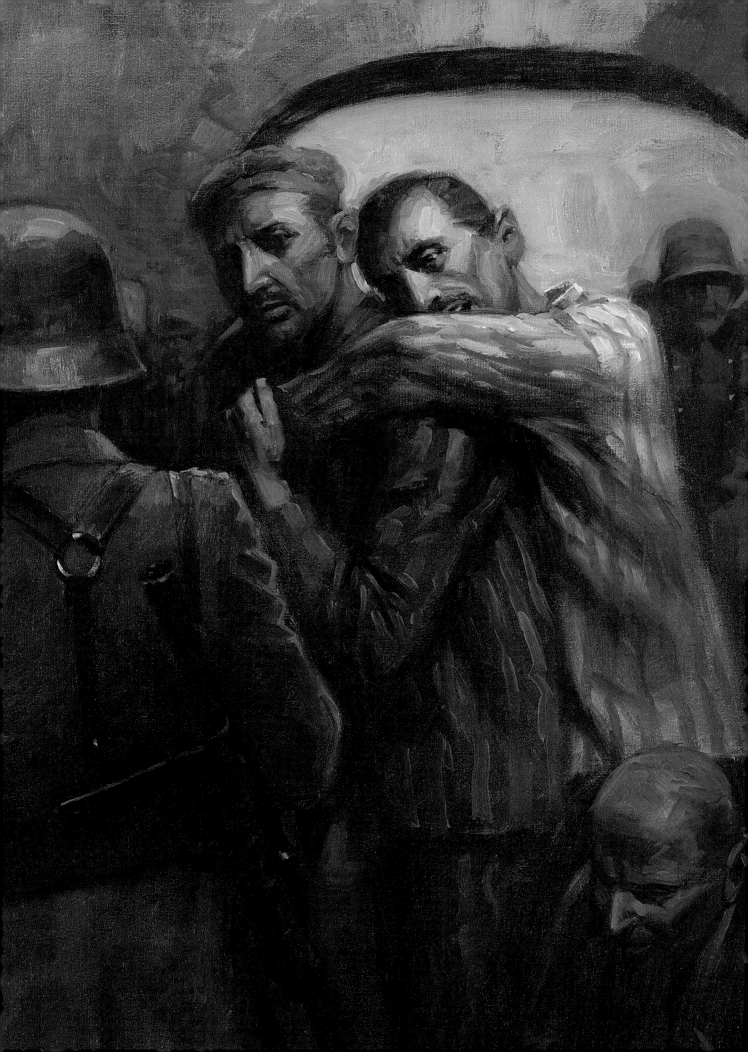

A couple of weeks later, Simon and other prisoners were taken into a courtyard at night to be executed when a roar sounded overhead. As Soviet planes started bombing, everyone ran for cover. The Soviet army was making headway into Poland. SS men took Simon and other prisoners back to Janowska.

From there the thirty-four remaining Jewish men and women were taken to the city of Przemsyl by freight car. But why were the SS taking Jews with them as they retreated? Two hundred SS men were using the prisoners as an excuse to avoid fighting the advancing Soviets. At Przemsyl they continued on foot. The SS men marched the prisoners through the woods, picking up hundreds of new prisoners along the way. Soon there were five hundred.

The forced march continued from camp to camp to the Gross-Rosen Concentration Camp, which was near a stone quarry. There Simon heard devastating news. A prisoner from Warsaw told him that the street where Cyla was hidden had been blown up in an explosion that no one could have survived. From then on Simon believed that his wife was dead.

Assigned to work barefoot in the stone quarry, Simon had his toe crushed when an SS man dropped a rock on his foot. His toe was amputated, and he hobbled about using a broomstick for support.

Fleeing the advancing Allied troops, the SS took Simon and other prisoners on another forced march to the Buchenwald Concentration Camp, where those who survived were loaded into open trucks in the snow. On February 9, 1945, they arrived at the Mauthausen Concentration Camp in Austria. By now Simon, who was five feet eleven inches tall, weighed only ninety-nine pounds. He was not expected to live and was assigned to the *death block*.

One day the kapo (a leader the SS picked from the prisoners) came in and asked if anyone could draw. "I can," Simon answered weakly. The kapo agreed to exchange another half portion of watery *nettle* soup per day for a drawing for a birthday present. "He brought me paper and pencils, and I began to draw," said Simon. "It helped me to forget where I was and took my mind off the dead and the dying people around me." More orders for drawings came in, bringing more food, which helped keep Simon alive.

On the morning of May 5, 1945, American troops reached Mauthausen and liberated the prisoners. The night before, the SS guards had run away. Now American soldiers took charge. They brought in medical supplies and kettles of "*real* soup." Although still very weak, Simon went to the War Crimes Office and offered his services. A lieutenant looked at him and laughingly told him to go back to his bunk and take it easy. But every day Simon returned and listened as American officers questioned suspected war criminals. "Just to get rid of me, they gave me pen and paper," he recalled, "and said write down all you know and then we'll think [about it] again. Back in my bunker I listed the camps where I had been, and the names of Nazis I remembered with their rank and number and their crimes." He also recorded the names of Nazis who had behaved well. Despite his weakened condition Simon still had a remarkable memory. His list contained ninety-one names. Twenty days later Simon was hired.

"I had no one anymore," he said. "No family, no friends." But helping the Americans gave him a purpose. "Someone had to live on and tell what it was really like."

In the months following liberation, Simon went with the Americans to Linz, Austria, to search for war criminals. Together with a few other survivors of Mauthausen, he set up a Jewish committee that helped former prisoners find their surviving families.

In the winter of 1945, he received thrilling news. Cyla was alive! "I'll never forget the moment when I saw Cyla's handwriting on the envelope," he said. "I read the letter so many times that I knew it by heart." Joyously he and Cyla reunited and the next year their daughter, Pauline Rose, was born. She was named for her two grandmothers, who had been killed. Affectionately Simon called her Paulinka.

When Paulinka started school, she realized that unlike her non-Jewish classmates she had no grandparents, aunts, uncles, or cousins. "Why don't we have relatives?" she asked. At first Simon couldn't bear to tell her about the Holocaust. "When she was eleven," he said, "I slowly began to tell her the whole truth." But, Paulinka later said, "I was not aware of the nature of my father's work."

In 1947 Simon opened the Historical Documentation Center in Linz. Simon's goal was to bring Nazi criminals to trial and leave a historical record of eyewitness accounts of Nazi crimes.

Simon needed to stay in Austria so he and his thirty volunteers could interview Holocaust survivors still in displaced persons camps. In the months just after the war, it was easier for him to track down Nazis. "If I pursued one Nazi, I would pick up three others on the way," he said. "I would receive heaps of letters with information, most of them sent anonymously."

But many Nazis had changed their names and gone into hiding. Some had fled to Argentina, Paraguay, Canada, and even the United States. Simon was determined to find them no matter how long it took. Still, he needed funding. He depended on contributions from people who had heard about his work. He also raised money himself by writing and giving lectures. Paulinka said, "He was an extremely busy man, active on many fronts at the same time."

Hundreds of testimonies from survivors arrived. Stacks of files cluttered his desk. Folders, binders, and more file boxes crowded the bookshelves. Yet Simon could instantly lay his hands on anything he needed. "One of my most important gifts," he said later, "is an almost photographic memory and a skill, like a computer's, for rapidly making all kinds of cross-links."

Since the late 1940s Simon had been hunting for one of the most wanted Nazi war criminals, Adolf Eichmann. "Eichmann was responsible for more murders than any other member of the Nazi Party," he said. For years Simon sifted through clues, tips, and information, uncovering secret organizations that helped former Nazis escape. By 1954 he had traced Eichmann to Buenos Aires, Argentina; but he ran out of money and had to give up.

Discouraged and disappointed, Simon closed his office in Linz in 1954. He packed up hundreds of pounds of files on 365 war criminals and sent the material to Yad Vashem, the Holocaust Martyrs' and Heroes' Remembrance Authority in Israel. Yet he kept one large file on Eichmann.

During the next few years, Simon worked with refugees, helping them learn vocational skills and teaching them languages. He also kept following the trails of Nazi criminals, particularly Eichmann.

In 1958 he took on the case that he considered top priority: finding the Gestapo officer who had arrested Anne Frank. Simon wondered where to start. "There was almost nothing to go on," he said.

Like any detective, he looked for clues, beginning with Anne's diary. Anne's last entry was dated August 1, 1944, three days before her arrest. Simon knew from Otto Frank's afterword in the diary that the officer who had arrested her had searched the annex for valuables. He had dumped out the contents of the briefcase where Anne kept her diary, leaving her writings scattered on the floor.

In the appendix of the published diary, Simon found the name of Victor Kugler, one of Otto's non-Jewish employees who had helped them while they were in hiding.

On the morning the Franks were arrested, Kugler had been working downstairs in the office. He also had been taken to Gestapo headquarters where he spoke up on behalf of the Franks.

Simon contacted Victor Kugler. Kugler remembered being questioned by the officer who had arrested the Franks, an Austrian SS man named Silvernagel. Simon knew that the name Silver did not exist in German. Kugler may have made a mistake in the translation. The word *silver* in Dutch and English was *silber* in German. Silbernagel was a common Austrian name, so Simon started looking through telephone books. "Seven people named Silbernagel were listed in the Vienna telephone directory," he said; "almost a hundred more were in various city registers. . . . If at least I knew the man's first name!"

Throughout his life Simon received threatening telephone calls and hate mail. That never stopped him. In 1960 Simon heard that Israeli agents had captured Eichmann in Argentina and had brought him to Israel to stand trial. He received a telegram from Yad Vashem that read, "Warmest congratulations on your brilliant success." He gave it to Paulinka and said, "Keep it for all those years I didn't have enough time to spend with you."

Inspired and encouraged, Simon turned his full attention to pursuing war criminals. In 1961 he, his wife, and his fifteen-year-old daughter moved to Vienna, and he opened a new documentation center in a dark, rundown apartment. There, among other cases, he carried on his search for the SS man named Silbernagel.

Simon knew that the man he was looking for had served in Holland with the Gestapo. Simon found eight men named Silbernagel who had been members of the Nazi Party and were the right age. Over the next few years, he investigated each one. "Rumors were sifted, facts checked," he said. "It was a long, tedious process, and I had to be extremely careful." His rule was to never bring charges against anyone without first gathering documentation. A friend helped him, and they even used private detectives. But none of the Silbernagels had arrested the Franks.

By 1963 Simon was stumped. "I came close to giving up the search," he recalled. "But then I remembered the arrogant face of the boys in Linz. I wanted them to go to their fathers and tell them: 'You lied; Anne Frank did exist. What other lies did you tell me?'"

He considered asking Anne's father, Otto, for help. Simon hesitated because he didn't want to upset this man "who had suffered so much," and he was afraid that Otto might ask him to stop his investigation. He knew that Otto had spoken out in favor of "forgiveness," for which German newspapers had praised him. Although Simon respected Otto's views, he said, "My conscience forces me to bring the guilty ones to trial."

At that point Dutch friends told Simon that the man he was looking for was probably named Silberthaler. He tracked down three such people, but none of them was the right one.

He started to lose hope.

On his next trip to Amsterdam, Simon talked to colleagues in the Netherlands Institute for War Documentation. They gave him a copy of the 1943 telephone directory of the Gestapo in Holland. It contained more than three hundred names. He decided to search for names that *looked* like Silberthaler during the flight back to Vienna. Just as he was about to doze off, he came to a page marked "IV Special Squad" and the subtitle "IV B4 *Joden* (Jews)." There were four names: Kempin, Buschmann, Scherf, and Silberbauer. All of a sudden "I was wide awake," recalled Simon. "I was sure this was my man." But where was he now?

At home, before taking off his coat, Simon went through the Vienna telephone book. His heart sank. There were twenty-six Silberbauers. And there might be more in other Austrian cities. It could take years to investigate each of them.

But Simon had a hunch. He figured that his man had probably worked for the Vienna police and might still. So he called a friend who was head of the Austrian Ministry of the Interior and had worked to expose Nazi war crimes. "I've found the Gestapo man who arrested Anne Frank," he said. "He's a Vienna policeman by the name of Silberbauer."

"What's his first name?" asked his friend.

Simon didn't know. His friend said there were six policemen with that last name. Simon wanted to look at the men's files. His friend told him to submit his request in writing.

On June 2, 1963, Simon mailed his request. Nothing happened. For the next five months, he was brushed off whenever he asked about it.

On November 11, the Austrian Communist Party newspaper ran a sensational story: Karl Silberbauer had been suspended from duty because he might have been involved with the Anne Frank case. Simon called his friend, who said there had been a leak. Silberbauer had been told to keep quiet; but when he was questioned, he said, "Yes, I arrested Anne Frank."

Simon immediately contacted a Dutch newspaper editor with the true story. It made front-page news throughout Europe and the United States. "Sleuthing Adds Two Footnotes to History," read a headline in *The New York Times*. "The Nazi officer who put an end to the diary of Anne Frank by arresting her and her family in 1944 has been identified as a Viennese police inspector. . . . Silberbauer was identified by a Jewish engineer, Simon Wiesenthal, head of the Jewish Documentation Center in Vienna."

Radio and television interviews followed. Otto Frank, who now lived in Switzerland, revealed that he had always known the name of the Gestapo policeman who had arrested them. But he had withheld the information because he appreciated the respect the policeman had shown upon discovering that Otto had been a German officer in World War I. "Perhaps he would have spared us if he had been by himself," said Otto.

Simon wanted to bring Silberbauer to trial, but Austrian authorities found no evidence that he was guilty of deporting the Franks and therefore could not try him as a war criminal. A review board cleared Silberbauer of any guilt regarding Anne Frank, and he returned to the Vienna police force. An official declared, "The Frank family was just one of many Jewish families who were rounded up by the Gestapo."

Simon gave Silberbauer's address to a Dutch reporter, who interviewed the policeman. "Why pick on me after all these years?" asked Silberbauer angrily. "I only did my duty."

During all those years Simon was looking for Silberbauer, he had been working at police headquarters, a ten-minute walk from Simon's office.

Simon never again saw the neo-Nazi teenager who had challenged him to find Silberbauer in the first place. "I should have liked one of those youngsters to come to me and say: 'Yes, Herr Wiesenthal, you have convinced me.' But that would have taken courage," he said. "And that, unfortunately, is what neo-Nazis lack."

However, the world knew about Silberbauer. Simon had proved that Anne Frank had lived and had written her diary. The publicity stirred up by the case had made the world remember the horror of the Holocaust. Many more cases followed as Simon continued hunting down infamous Nazi war criminals and bringing them to court.

When a fellow survivor from Mauthausen congratulated Simon on his detective work, he said, "If you had gone back to building houses, you'd be a millionaire. Why didn't you?"

Simon replied, "When we come to the other world and meet the millions of Jews who died in the camps and they ask us, 'What have you done?' there will be many answers. . . . But I will say, 'I didn't forget you.'"

Simon Wiesenthal 1908–2005

Simon Wiesenthal was born on December 31, 1908, in Buczacz, Galicia. At that time Galicia was part of the Austro-Hungarian Empire; today it is part of Ukraine. Simon was two when his brother, Hillel, was born. Their father, Asher, traded in wholesale goods, mainly sugar; and Simon liked to build houses out of sugar cubes at his father's warehouse. When World War I broke out, in 1914, Asher was called up for active duty in the Austro-Hungarian army and killed in action in 1915.

During the war, Russian Cossacks invaded Buczacz and attacked Jews. Simon's mother, Rosa, fled with him and his brother to Vienna, Austria, where Simon and Hillel attended school. By 1917 the Russians left Buczacz, so Simon, now nine, and his family returned. For a while Galicia became part of Ukraine, then the Polish army invaded. World War I ended in 1918 with the defeat of Germany, but Galicia kept changing hands. "We would get up in the morning without knowing what regime was in power," remembered Simon. When he was twelve, Ukrainian soldiers stormed the town. A soldier on horseback chased Simon and stabbed his thigh with a sword. Simon recovered but had a scar for the rest of his life.

In 1923, at age fifteen, Simon entered high school and met Cyla Muller. He was leader of a Boy Scout group but refused to wear a uniform. The year Simon started high school, his brother fell and broke his back. The accident paralyzed Hillel, and he died a few months later. By 1926 Simon's mother remarried; and she and her new husband moved to Dolina, in the foothills of the Carpathian Mountains. Simon stayed behind to finish high school and lived with Cyla's family. Upon graduating, Simon decided to study architecture. Although he wanted to go to the univer-

sity in nearby L'vov, the city was under Polish rule, and few Jews were accepted. Instead Simon went to the Czech Technical College in Prague. At age twenty-four he passed his exams and went to L'vov to complete his studies. Jews were still not welcome, but the university accepted him. Simon also took a job with a local building firm and began designing houses.

During this period Adolf Hitler came to power. In 1933 Hitler became chancellor of Germany and established the first concentration camps. In 1935 he passed the Nuremberg Laws, classifying Jews, Gypsies, and blacks as a threat to "racial purity." In 1936 Simon, age twenty-eight, married Cyla. When World War II began in 1939, the Germans invaded Galicia.

Simon and Cyla were sent to the Janowska Con-

ABOVE: *Simon Wiesenthal speaking in Israel at funeral services for unknown death camp victims. He had accompanied their ashes.*

LEFT: *Simon Wiesenthal, age fifteen, in suit and tie (front row center), with his group of Boy Scouts in Buczacz, Poland*

centration Camp near L'vov in 1941. That year, on December 7, Japan bombed the American military base at Pearl Harbor, Hawaii, and the United States entered the war. In 1942 Hitler began "the Final Solution," his plan to exterminate the Jews of Europe.

By the time the war ended in 1945, Simon had miraculously survived twelve concentration camps. He and Cyla were reunited and discovered they had lost eighty-nine members of their families in the Holocaust. In 1946 their daughter, Paulinka, was born.

In 1947 Simon opened his Historical Documentation Center in Linz, Austria. His wife begged him to forget the past and move to Israel, proclaimed a homeland for Jews in 1948. Simon refused, and Cyla stayed with him. The onset of the cold war between the United States and the Soviet Union in the early 1950s dulled interest in pursuing and prosecuting war criminals. The United States and its allies were more concerned with helping West Germany rebuild its army. Simon closed his office in Linz in 1954 for lack of funds and devoted his time to writing. His book *I Hunted Eichmann,* published in 1961 when he was fifty-three, made him famous and revived interest in his work. Simon moved with his wife and daughter to Vienna and opened a new documentation center. Although he described himself as a "one-man band," he occasionally hired part-time help in his office. Rosa-Maria Austraat came to work for him as a secretary in 1975 and stayed for the rest of his life as his office manager. Simon was brilliantly organized and relentless in his efforts, yet friends and colleagues

described him as warm, cheerful, and a great story-teller who loved to laugh and tell jokes.

Over the years he brought more than 1,100 Nazi war criminals to justice all over the world. Not everyone applauded his efforts. After a bomb planted by neo-Nazis exploded at his home in Vienna in 1982, tenants of his office building signed a petition forcing him to move; and the neo-Nazi World Union of National Socialists put a price on his head—dead, not alive. Nevertheless, Simon carried on his crusade and kept working well into his nineties. He received medals and awards from countries all over the world. In 2003, the year his wife died, Simon's health declined and he retired. He died at home in Vienna in 2005 at the age of ninety-six.

ABOVE: *Simon and Cyla Wiesenthal in 1936, the year they were married*
LEFT: *Simon Wiesenthal and the Dalai Lama discussing their philosophies, 1993*
BELOW: *Simon Wiesenthal, 1993*

Resources

BOOKS

Bartoletti, Susan Campbell. *Hitler Youth: Growing Up in Hitler's Shadow.* New York: Scholastic, 2005.

Italia, Robert. *Courageous Crimefighters.* Minneapolis: The Oliver Press, Inc., 1995.

Jeffrey, Laura S. *Simon Wiesenthal: Tracking Down Nazi Criminals.* Springfield, NJ: Enslow Publishers, Inc., 1997.

Levy, Alan. *Nazi Hunter: The Wiesenthal File.* New York: Carroll & Graf Publishers, 2002.

Noble, Iris. *Nazi Hunter: Simon Wiesenthal.* New York: Julian Messner, 1979.

Pick, Hella. *Simon Wiesenthal: A Life in Search of Justice.* Boston: Northeastern University Press, 1996.

Rogasky, Barbara. *Smoke and Ashes: The Story of the Holocaust,* Revised and Expanded Edition. New York: Holiday House, 2002.

Wechsberg, Joseph, editor. *The Murderers Among Us: The Wiesenthal Memoirs.* New York: McGraw-Hill Book Company, 1967.

Wiesenthal, Simon. *The Sunflower: On the Possibilities and Limits of Forgiveness,* Revised and Expanded Edition. New York: Schocken Books, 1998.

———. *Justice Not Vengeance.* New York: Grove Weidenfeld, 1989.

UNPUBLISHED PAPERS

Kentaro Hishihara. "Visiting Mr. Simon Wiesenthal." Tokyo: Japan, 1997.

Simon Wiesenthal Testimony/Shoah Foundation, Visual History Foundation. Place of interview, Vienna 14, Austria, November 1997. Translator and editor: Annemarie Bestor, volunteer, Simon Wiesenthal Center Library, 2006.

ARTICLES

Blumenthal, Ralph. "Simon Wiesenthal Is Dead at 96; Tirelessly Pursued Nazi Fugitives." *The New York Times,* September 21, 2005.

Farnsworth, Clyde A. "Sleuth with Six Million Clients." *The New York Times Magazine,* February 2, 1964.

Hier, Rabbi Marvin. "Simon Wiesenthal: A Man of the Generations." *Response World Report,* Simon Wiesenthal Center, Snider Social Action Institute, Fall/Winter 2005, Vol. 26.

"Sleuthing Adds Two Footnotes to History." *The New York Times,* November 21, 1963.

Weinstein, Henry. "Nazi Hunter Loyal to the Dead." *Los Angeles Times,* September 21, 2005.

VIDEOS

The Art of Remembrance: Simon Wiesenthal. Written and directed by Johanna Heer and Werner Schmiedel. Coproduced by ORF/River Lights Pictures, Inc., 1994.

The Century of Simon Wiesenthal. The Willy Lindwer Collection. Written, produced, and directed by Willy Lindwer. Dutch with English subtitles. AVA Productions BV, 1994; Ergo Media Inc., 1995.

I Have Never Forgotten You: The Life and Legacy of Simon Wiesenthal. Written by Rick Trank and Rabbi Marvin Hier. Directed by Rick Trank. Produced by Moriah Films, 2006.

CORRESPONDENCE

E-mail notes from Paulinka Wiesenthal Kreisberg, March 7, 2007; March 17, 2007; March 29, 2007; and April 17, 2007.

E-mail from Trudi Mergili, Dokumentationszentrum des Bundes Judischer Verfolgter des Naziregimes, Simon Wiesenthal Archives, April 24, 2007.

Fax from Rosa-Maria Austraat, Simon Wiesenthal's longtime secretary and close associate in Vienna; and copies of the Documentation Center's annual reports, March 5, 2007.

Glossary

Aryan – The Nazis applied the term to people with a northern European racial background who were often tall, blond, and blue eyed. Hitler believed that Aryans were a superior, or "master," race.

concentration camp – Prison camps without adequate food, water, sanitation, clothing—necessities of life—where Nazis sent all "enemies of the Third Reich," people they thought were dangerous to their plans. Jews were the largest single group imprisoned.

death block – A building, Block VI in Mauthausen Concentration Camp, where the SS sent prisoners who were too weak or sick to work. Room A was "better"; Room B was for those who were expected to die immediately. Simon Wiesenthal was put in Room A.

forced-labor camp – A type of concentration camp where the Nazis sent people to be used as slave laborers and worked them to death. Living conditions and brutality of the guards made survival almost impossible. All camps were supervised by the SS, Hitler's private army.

forgery – The crime of falsely signing another person's name to a document or piece of writing or passing off as authentic a report, story, or official paper written by someone else as one's own.

Gestapo – The Secret State Police established in April 1933 by Hermann Goering. The Gestapo had total freedom to arrest, interrogate, and deport Jews, Gypsies, homosexuals, and anyone else considered an enemy of the Third Reich.

ghetto – A section or street where Jews were forced to live behind barbed wires, walls, or fences, set off from the population around them. The ghettos were eventually liquidated and the Jews were deported to extermination camps.

neo-Nazis – Members of contemporary hate groups who call themselves Nazis and praise Hitler as the savior of the "Aryan" race. Some call themselves "skinheads" and "white supremacists" and commit violent hate crimes.

nettle – A plant covered with stinging hairs like needles that is used for food.

partisans – Members of underground resistance groups operating within and behind enemy lines during World War II. They hid in forests and helped other escapees from ghettos and concentration camps, and together fought the Nazis.

restitution money – Money paid by governments, mainly Germany, to Jews to compensate for the injuries, damages, and losses they suffered during the Holocaust.

SS – Schutzstaffel, meaning "Protection Squad." Formed in 1925 as Hitler's personal bodyguard, it was transformed into a giant organization. Members wore a skull and crossbones on their caps and collars.

swastikas – Ancient symbols that often meant good luck. The swastika became the symbol of Nazism and was used on the German flag.

Ukrainian – Pertaining to the Ukraine, a republic in Eastern Europe that is bordered by Russia on the north and east, and Poland and Hungary on the west. During World War II, the Ukraine was part of the Soviet Union.

Index

Page numbers in *italics* refer to photographs.

Acknowledgments

When I read of Simon Wiesenthal's death in 2005, I knew that I wanted to pay tribute to him and his work. I was fortunate enough to correspond with him in 2000 while doing a book about Mauthausen Concentration Camp. This came about because of my association with the Simon Wiesenthal Center and Museum of Tolerance Library & Archives. Therefore, I first want to thank Adaire J. Klein, Director of Library and Archival Services; Fama Mor, former Archivist and Curator; Nancy Saul, Reference and Information Services librarian; and the Library and Archives staff and volunteers of the Simon Wiesenthal Center Museum of Tolerance for helping me with research.

Adaire and Fama put me in touch with Rosa-Maria Austraat, who worked closely with Simon Wiesenthal in the Vienna Documentation Center for many years. I thank Rosa-Maria Austraat for providing me with information and for referring me to Trudi Mergili at the Simon Wiesenthal Archives in Vienna. I am deeply grateful to Simon Wiesenthal's daughter, Paulinka Wiesenthal Kreisberg, for generously taking the time to answer some of my questions by e-mail.

At Holiday House I am grateful to my editor, Mary Cash, who worked miracles in helping me shape this book. And a big thank you to her assistant, Pamela Glauber.

As always I am indebted to George Nicholson, agent, mentor, and friend, for his guidance, and to his assistant, Emily Hazel.

A special thank you to Kimberly Retts and the Institute on Law, Religion & Ethics at Pepperdine School of Law in Malibu, California, for graciously allowing me to view the documentary film *I Have Never Forgotten You: The Life and Legacy of Simon Wiesenthal* before its commercial release.

Lastly, enormous thanks to my writer friends, Lunch Bunch, for their critiques and support.

In memory of Simon Wiesenthal (1908–2005)
His legacy lives on for all humanity. —S. G. R.

For the Briggs family —B. F.

Text copyright © 2009 by Susan Goldman Rubin
Illustrations copyright © 2009 by Bill Farnsworth
All Rights Reserved
Printed and Bound in China
www.holidayhouse.com
First Edition
1 3 5 7 9 10 8 6 4 2

Library of Congress Cataloging-in-Publication Data
Rubin, Susan Goldman.
The Anne Frank case : Simon Wiesenthal's search for the truth /
by Susan Goldman Rubin ; illustrated by Bill Farnsworth. — 1st ed.
p. cm.
ISBN-13: 978-0-8234-2109-1 (hardcover)
1. Wiesenthal, Simon—Juvenile literature. 2. Jews—Austria—
Biography—Juvenile literature. 3. Holocaust survivors—Austria—
Biography—Juvenile literature. 4. Nazi hunters—
Austria—Biography—Juvenile literature. 5. Holocaust, Jewish (1939-
1945)—Juvenile literature. 6. Austria—Biography.
I. Farnsworth, Bill. II. Title. • DS135.A93W536 2009
940.53'18092—dc22 • [B] • 2007028396

Source Notes

The following notes refer to the sources of quoted material. Each citation includes the first and last words or phrases of the quotation and the source. Unless otherwise noted, references are to works cited in the Resources on page 38.

p. 3: "Can you come . . . It's a fake!" Simon Wiesenthal quoted in Wechsberg, p. 172

p. 6: "When I arrived . . . them." Ibid., p. 173

p. 6: "It was just . . . having fun." Ibid., p. 173

p. 7: "but their . . . teachers." Ibid., p. 173

p. 9: "Fritz . . . during the demonstration?" Ibid., p. 175

p. 9: "Yes, of course . . . Wiesenthal the Nazi hunter." Simon Wiesenthal quoted in *The Century of Simon Wiesenthal*

p. 9: "Wiesenthal, Austria." Levy, p. 9

p. 9: "What about . . . himself admitted to it." Simon Wiesenthal quoted in Wechsberg, pp. 175–176

p. 9: "We'll accept . . . not from you." Simon Wiesenthal quoted in *The Century of Simon Wiesenthal*

p. 9: "I had to find . . . years before." Simon Wiesenthal quoted in Wechsberg, p. 176

p. 10: "We stood . . . enough for today." Simon Wiesenthal quoted in *The Art of Remembrance: Simon Wiesenthal*

p. 14: "We need Wiesenthal." Simon Wiesenthal quoted in Wechsberg, p. 34

p. 14: "We need . . . birthday celebrations." Simon Wiesenthal quoted in Pick, p. 62

p. 14: "For a long . . . in miracles." Simon Wiesenthal quoted in Levy, p. 49

p. 14: "I wrote down . . . I knew." Simon Wiesenthal quoted in *The Art of Remembrance*

p. 18: "I can." Simon Wiesenthal quoted in Levy, p. 75

p. 18: "He brought me . . . people around me." Simon Wiesenthal quoted in Wechsberg, p. 44

p. 18: "*real* soup." Ibid., p. 46

p. 18: "Just to get . . . and their crimes." Simon Wiesenthal quoted in Pick, p. 84

p. 18: "I had no one . . . no friends." Simon Wiesenthal quoted in *The Century of Simon Wiesenthal*

p. 18: "Someone had to live . . . really like." Simon Wiesenthal quoted in Farnsworth, p. 11

p. 20: "I'll never forget . . . by heart." Simon Wiesenthal quoted in Wechsberg, p. 54

p. 20: "Why don't . . . whole truth." Simon Wiesenthal quoted in *I Have Never Forgotten You*

p. 20: "I was not . . . father's work." Paulinka Kreisberg quoted in *I Have Never Forgotten You*

p. 21: "If I pursued . . . sent anonymously." Simon Wiesenthal quoted in Pick, p. 99

p. 22: "He was . . . the same time." Paulinka Kreisberg quoted in *I Have Never Forgotten You*

p. 22: "One of my . . . cross-links." Simon Wiesenthal quoted in Wiesenthal, *Justice Not Vengeance*, p. 294

p. 22: "Eichmann was . . . Nazi Party." Simon Wiesenthal quoted in *I Have Never Forgotten You*

p. 25: "There was . . . to go on." Simon Wiesenthal quoted in Wechsberg, p. 176

p. 26: "Seven people . . . first name!" Ibid., p. 177

p. 26: "Warmest congratulations . . . spend with you." Simon Wiesenthal quoted in *I Have Never Forgotten You*

p. 26: "Rumors were sifted . . . extremely careful." Simon Wiesenthal quoted in Wechsberg, p. 177

p. 29: "I came close . . . you tell me?" Ibid., p. 177

p. 29: "who had suffered . . . ones to trial." Ibid., pp. 178–179

p. 30: "IV Special Squad"; "IV . . . (Jews.)." Ibid., p. 180

p. 30: "I was wide . . . my man." Simon Wiesenthal quoted in Wiesenthal, *Justice Not Vengeance*, p. 339

p. 30: "I've found . . . name of Silberbauer." Ibid., p. 339

p. 30: "What's his first name?" Ibid., p. 173

p. 32: "Yes, I arrested Anne Frank." Karl Silberbauer quoted in Farnsworth, "Sleuth with Six Million Clients"

p. 32: "Sleuthing Adds . . . Center in Vienna." "Sleuthing Adds Two Footnotes to History," p. 41

p. 33: "Perhaps he . . . by himself." Otto Frank quoted in Carol Ann Lee, *The Hidden Life of Otto Frank* (New York: Viking/Penguin, 2002), p. 264

p. 34: "The Frank family . . . by the Gestapo." Official of the Austrian Interior Ministry quoted in "Sleuthing Adds Two Footnotes to History," p. 41

p. 34: "Why pick . . . my duty." Karl Silberbauer quoted in Wechsberg, p. 182

p. 34: "I should have liked . . . neo-Nazis lack." Simon Wiesenthal quoted in Wiesenthal, *Justice Not Vengeance*, p. 340

p. 34: "If you . . . Why didn't you?" Wiesenthal's camp mate from Mauthausen quoted in Farnsworth, p. 11

p. 34: "When we come . . . 'I didn't forget you.'" Simon Wiesenthal quoted in Farnsworth, p. 11

p. 37: "one-man band." Simon Wiesenthal quoted in Pick, p. 273